Before Columbus

Written and Illustrated by Muriel Batherman

Houghton Mifflin Company   Boston   1981

For Carla Stevens

Library of Congress Cataloging-in-Publication Data

Batherman, Muriel.
 Before Columbus.
 Summary: Describes the dwellings, tools, clothing, customs, and other aspects of
daily life of the earliest inhabitants of North America, the Basketmaker Indians and
their descendants the Pueblos, as revealed through archaeological exploration.
 ISBN 0-395-30088-6
 1. Basket-Maker Indians—Juvenile literature. 2. Pueblos—Juvenile literature.
[1. Basket-Maker Indians. 2. Pueblos. 3. Indians of North America]   I. Title.
E99.B37B37   80-19621
970.01'1

Printed in the United States of America

RNF ISBN 0-395-30088-6
PAP ISBN 0-395-54954-X

WOZ 10 9 8 7 6 5 4 3

CONTENTS

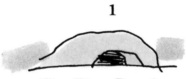
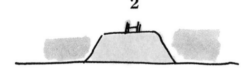
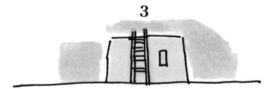

1

The First People

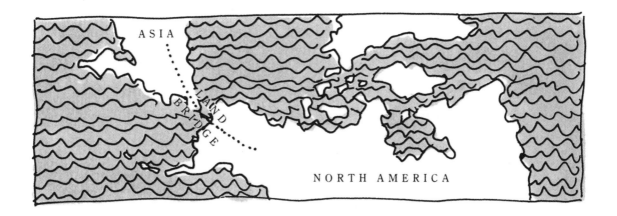

Many thousands of years ago, a strip of dry land connected Asia and North America. The land formed a bridge between the two continents. People could walk from one continent to the other. Hunters from Asia crossed this bridge to North America. Soon the hunters began to hunt the bison and mammoths that roamed the plains of North America in those days. Many tribes of hunters followed. Then gradually the land bridge was covered by the ocean, and water separated the two lands.

These hunters were the first discoverers of North America. They wandered in search of food. They lived on the plants and wildlife of the new land. As they hunted some drifted to the Southwestern part of North America. There is very little rain in this part of North America, which now includes the states of Utah, New Mexico, Arizona, and Colorado. The dry climate in this area helped preserve some of the things the hunters left behind thousands of years ago.

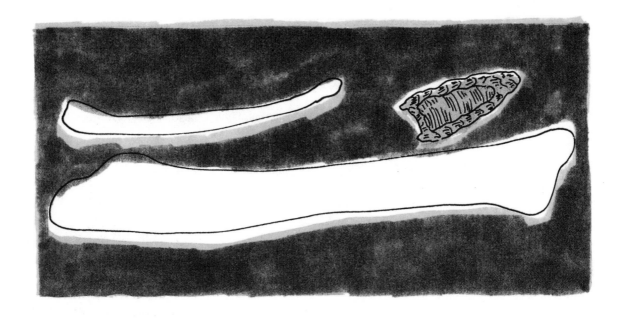

The hunters left their hunting weapons behind. Parts of these weapons were discovered in New Mexico. Spear points were found among the bones of a breed of bison that lived more than 10,000 years ago. The points were carefully shaped pieces of stone made to kill animals. The discovery of these weapons was the first clue that there had been hunters in North America in the days when these animals lived.

Other discoveries were made in the Southwest. Cowboys found caves with walls blackened from fires. The early hunters used the caves for warmth and shelter. There were bones of animals and spear points scattered in the dust and ashes on the floors of the caves.
Under the dust and ashes was the most important discovery of all.

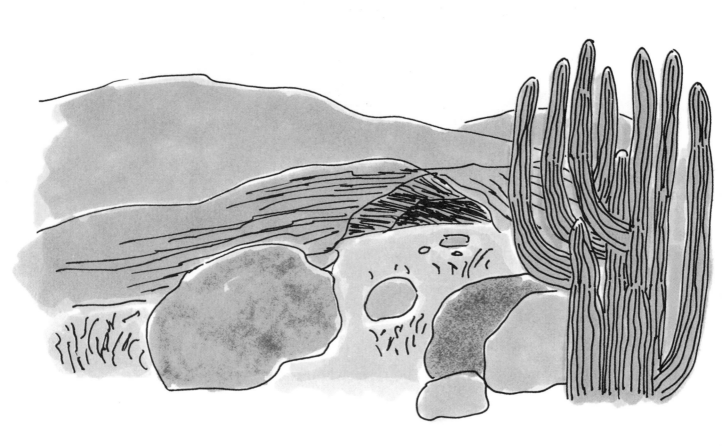

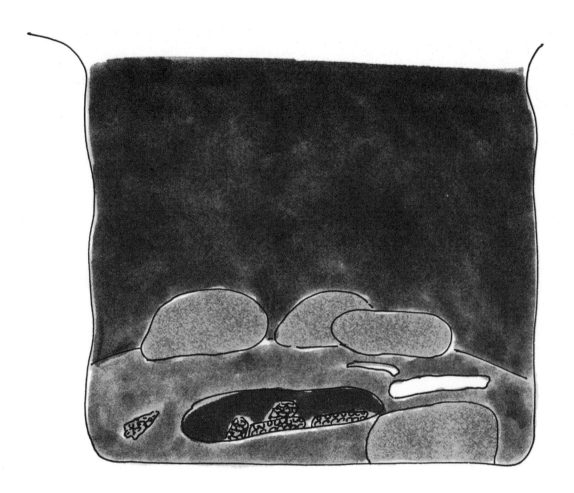

There were holes dug in the floors of the caves. Some of the holes were storage pits for food. Others were burial places.

Some holes contained skeletons of people. The buried skeletons were wrapped in blankets of fur. Large numbers of tightly woven baskets were buried with the skeletons. The baskets suggested a name for the people buried with them. The people were called the Basketmakers.

Skeletons and baskets were not the only things found in the caves. There were other things as well. Many of the Basketmakers' personal belongings were found buried in the trash that remained. From the things the Basketmakers left behind, we can guess how they lived.

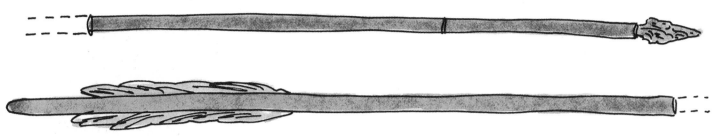

The Basketmakers left spear-throwers behind. They were wooden
weapons made to kill animals smaller and faster than the bisons.
The Basketmakers' spear-thrower came in two parts. One part was the
holder. The holder had rawhide loops for the hunter's fingers to fit
through. It also had a grooved notch for a six-foot spear to rest in. One
end of the spear was tipped with a small stone point. The opposite
end had feathers.

They left sandals behind. The Basketmakers made sandals to protect their feet from the hot, dry land. The sandals were made from yucca plant fibers. The fibers were woven into cord. The cord formed the sole of the sandal. A heel and toe loop held the sandal in place.

The Basketmakers left hair ornaments and necklaces behind.
The hair ornaments were pieces of bone that were shaped to a point
and tied together. Some of the ornaments were topped with feathers.
Their necklaces were made of seeds, acorn cups, shells, and pieces
of bone strung together.

They left long, pointed, wooden sticks behind. From these sticks we know that the Basketmakers were farmers as well as hunters. The sticks were used for planting corn, beans, and squash.

They left baskets behind. The Basketmakers wove them from yucca plant fibers in many different sizes and shapes. There were trays and bowls. There were small baskets used for storage and larger baskets used for food gathering and carrying water. The water baskets were lined with a gum-like material taken from trees. The gum lining prevented the water from seeping out.

The Basketmakers also cooked in their water baskets. They did this by adding hot stones to the water. When the stones cooled the people would replace them until the water was hot enough for cooking.

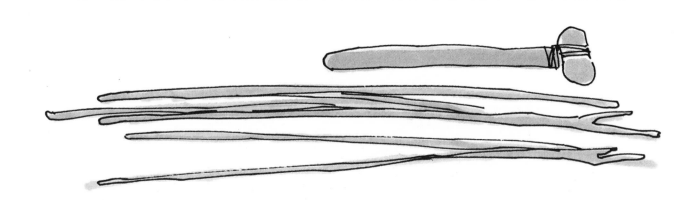

The Basketmakers lived in caves for several hundred years.
During this time the people became better farmers. Their crops produced
larger harvests. They learned how to store the food they grew.
Farming became more important than hunting. When this happened,
the Basketmakers' living habits changed. They no longer had to keep
moving to follow the animals for food. The Basketmakers stopped living
in caves and began to build houses.

The Basketmakers left pit houses behind. These houses were built by digging shallow pits in the earth. Four log posts were placed in the corners to support a mud and grass roof. Small branches covered with mud formed the walls of the pit house.

About the time the Basketmakers were building their pit houses they also learned to make pottery. They made their pottery from clay. They formed the clay into a thin rope. Then they wound it in a circle. Each new rope of clay was attached to the one before it to form a bowl. Some of the pots had crude designs painted on them. They used their pottery for cooking.

4

The Pueblos, 750–1300 A.D.

Later the Basketmakers replaced the pit house with a larger dwelling. They left villages behind. They are called *pueblos,* a Spanish word for villages. The people living in the villages were given the same name. The Pueblos' first village had small flat-roofed houses that were joined together around an open court. The houses were built from sun-baked clay called *adobe.* The villages had enough rooms for many families. They were built close to the fields where the Pueblos grew their crops.

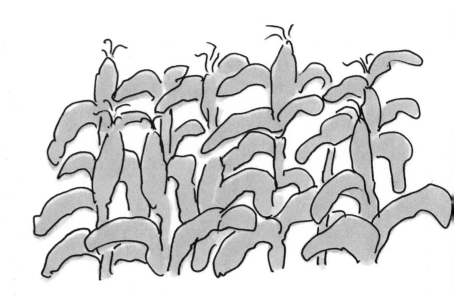

As the number of Pueblo families increased, more dwellings
were needed. The Pueblos left a city behind. The city was built under
the overhang of a huge cliff. It had apartment houses several stories high,
with rooms for hundreds of people. The houses were built from pieces
of stone that were cut and placed in layers and cemented with adobe.
Wooden ladders were used to reach the upper stories. The houses
had connecting rooms with walls, windows, and doors. There were also
storage rooms for food, round rooms for religious rites, and tall towers.

29

No one knows why the Pueblos left their cities. Perhaps there was a long dry period and they could not grow enough food. Perhaps an enemy forced them to leave. Smaller groups of Pueblos drifted to other parts of the Southwest. The builders of the cliff dwellings never built another city again.

The early hunters were the first people of North America. They came to hunt. Later, their descendants learned to plant crops and build houses. The hunters and their descendants respected their new land. They took from it only the things they needed to live. The things they left behind tell us about life in North America before Columbus.